Nestled in Memory

By James Levin

Gotham Books

30 N Gould St.
Ste. 20820, Sheridan, WY 82801
https://gothambooksinc.com/

Phone: 1 (307) 464-7800

© 2024 *James Levin*. All rights reserved.

No part of this book may be reproduced, stored in a retrieval system, or transmitted by any means without the written permission of the author.

Published by Gotham Books (August 28, 2024)

ISBN: 979-8-3303-9922-2 (H)
ISBN: 979-8-3303-7685-8 (P)
ISBN: 979-8-3303-7686-5 (E)

Because of the dynamic nature of the Internet, any web addresses or links contained in this book may have changed since publication and may no longer be valid.

The views expressed in this work are solely those of the author and do not necessarily reflect the views of the publisher, and the publisher hereby disclaims any responsibility for them.

To my sons Aaron, Sam, and Harry

And to the people today who are trying to love and not hate.

Contents

Bell 1

A Bride 2

A Medical Procedure 3

Diaphanous 4

Dreamland 5

Fire Stoking Fire 7

He Was Alone 8

Hospital Housing 10

How Can You Survive 11

Imperfection 13

Initiative Is 14

Love 15

Ordering Coffee 17

The Tympani 18

When You Look Behind 19

You Told Me 20

Looking Backward 21

A Door 23

A Siren 24

A Sparkling Whiff 25

A Student 26

A Wintery Place 27

Bird Song 28

Peering Into the Past 29

Phil 30

Questions 32

She is the Captain	33
The Sky	35
Scratchings	36
F-Words	37
Surprise	38
The Surface	39
Peering Outward	40
Faults	41
Spectacles	42
Look East	43
That Lake	44
My Swing	45
Reluctance	46
On Snow	47
In Normandy	48
Hanukkah	49
Around the Corner	50
A Short Poem	51
The Laugh	52
Hands and Words	53
The Booth	54
Fear	56
Searching	57
Contained	58
Peaks	59
Goodbye	60
Hmm...	61
Time	62
A Nine Eleven Memory	64

A Swoop A Quiver 65
Assets and Liabilities 66
Betsey 67
Blade of Truth 69

Two roads diverged in a wood, and I-
I took the one less traveled by,
And that has made all the difference.

-Robert Frost, "The Road Not Taken"

Bell

A bell
rings in the hills
says Paul.
Its sound is
deceptively sweet
like mint.
It is auburn
and curved,
carved from
God's earth.
That bell
rings sings sighs
soothes and smooths
atmospheric agitation,
earthquake tremors,
terrors and tremendous
expansiveness.
Silence.
Be silent.
Cooling breezes
bring wafts
of sound.
That bell
is precious
says Paul.

A Bride

She approaches
held by the men
she loves.
A bride
stands and faces
her beloved
clasping hands.
Faces of family and friends
adore them.
Surrounded by greenery
a steady breeze
crisp white chairs,
we share this moment.
Her mother watches
from a distance
perched on heaven's hill
nodding her blessing.
Rings are exchanged
on tremulous hands,
a glass is smashed
never to be reassembled.
And then the kiss of marriage
and then one more.
Her smile
touches the pinnacle of joy.

A Medical Procedure

She has the future
before her-
marriage,
a move to a new home,
a medical procedure.
The doctors say
the mass is this or that
but the devil could be
living within.
A minor operation
could become
a throat squeezing choke hold.
Bad news
might rip away
all her beauty and hope.
Satan lives as abnormal cells
multiplying insidiously
indifferent and oblivious to
dreams of dresses
and the flavor
of cake.
She will cross a bridge
this week.
What we think
will become
what we know.
The wedding and the move
will lunge ahead
or fall back
upon themselves.

Diaphanous

Her diaphanous nightgown
swishes against
her nipple-tipped
breasts,
falls past
her belly
and hemispheric bottom.
A sensation of air
she feels and smells
permeates the room.
She stands near
a darkened window,
light emits
from behind her,
outlines her
mountains and valleys
and soft plains.
She is a wisp,
a breath.
Diaphonous.

Dreamland

One night
a fine feeling of madness
meandered meaningfully
through each corpuscle
of his bloodstream.
There was a scream.
He sat bolt upright
searching the dusky darkness
with open shut eyes
wondering if that sound
was imagination,
inner reverberation
or his spouse's consternation.
Lying down,
placing his head upon the pillow,
like an embracing willow
enveloping him,
he swooshes back
into dreamland.
Red rollercoasters
smash into a fireworks
conflagration.
The glittering sparkling
eruptions
illuminate inner recesses,
stimulate neuronal interactions,
bring him above himself
like in a bunkbed
where he occupies

the upper and lower spaces.
He feels alarm,
alarm as his state of mind
collapses down into itself.
His eyes open now
upon an excruciating morning.
Mourning dreamland's demise,
sitting up,
placing his feet on the floor,
as his wife breathes in peace,
truth washes over him.
Flotsam and jetsam
are jettisoned away.
The day begins.

Fire Stoking Fire

When he looks
at her face
he sees those
rounded lips
and wishes
to kiss them,
to envelope them
within his own.
He would like
to hold and squeeze
her hand,
pull her towards
him.
Fire stoking fire,
expressing
a pleasure
beyond words.

He Was Alone

When he looked up,
after his eyes opened,
he was surprised
to be alive.
After the conundrums,
like elephants
had stampeded over his body,
after every nerve ending
had been stretched
crushed mangled maimed,
he never expected to see
God's blue sky again.
Lying there,
alone,
free of attachments
of any kind,
free of past words
deeds or actions,
free even of pain,
he began to float,
to float away,
away from his
tattered body and soul.
He went upward,
upward to a place,
a place he never knew existed,
a place of satisfactions
and understandings.
Looking downward

he saw that tattered body.
He sighed and cried for himself
and the others who believed
he was something he wasn't.
Floating still,
he saw the lovely nuances
trances and tracks
of the universe.
Now amongst the stars
he feared never returning
being only a wisp of memory
in the minds of so few.
Suddenly the dream evaporated,
his feet hit hard,
his knees buckled and bent,
he was prone once more.
He blinked.
He took a breath.
He was alone.

Hospital Housing

What happens
when a beautiful morning,
pristine perfection,
invites you seductively
to caress its
crisp luminosity.
You agree.
What happens
when that morning
is viewed through
institutional glass,
hospital housing.
The invitation
is withdrawn.
Your pain and situation
exclude you from participation.
As I step out
into exquisite indifference
and feel the solar expression,
I think of your expression,
your barrier,
your limitation.
I double my pleasure
to include you.

How Can You Survive

How can you survive
when you lose
what you love
the most?
House of Flying Daggers
turns a man's head.
Riding headlong headstrong
down a path
away from a woman
who has entered your
bloodstream,
been injected into
your soul.
You stop.
You halt,
your head ringing,
wringing your brain.
So you turn,
you turn towards
that most beautiful
of objects,
rare and rarefied
an exquisite jewel.
You race towards her,
your decision is made,
all prior doubts
and concerns
dissipate like dust
created as you ride.

You run like a happy fool
towards those lips
that nose
those eyes
that hair
that warmth.
As you arrive
the smell of death
permeates the air.
Blood replaces
the milk of passion,
the heat of your beloved
cools in your arms
as you surge forward
to meet her
in a last embrace.
How can love die?
How can you survive
when you lose
what you love
the most?

Imperfection

Baseball
played by
twelve-year-olds
deifies imperfection.
Their uniforms,
crisp red and white,
delineate the possibility
of excellence and precision,
like reaching to the right
to backhand a smacked ground ball,
then setting,
sending a line drive throw
to first.
The first baseman
stretches legs, arms, heart
to snag the ball
in his leather glove
before the charging runner's toe
touches the bag.
A pitcher
panting,
sweat bubbling
on his countenance,
counted on by teammates,
throws that third strike,
and welcomes victory.
Sometimes twelve-year-olds
play the game this way.
Sometimes they don't.

Initiative Is

Initiative is
assembling a tent
at one-twenty a.m.
when most twelve-year-olds
are sound asleep.
Was it the frappuccino
he drank earlier in the day?
Or is this compact
curly-haired son of ours
a little bit out of the ordinary.
Initiative is
taking a handful of life
and molding a vision
that others don't see
especially his mom and dad.
So the tent stands
and creativity pulses inwardly.
Steinbeck refers to
the black fear parents feel
for their children.
Initiative is
biting life
and hoping that the bite back
doesn't slash and burn.

Love

Love teeters
on a high wire
barely in view.
Above alone
holding that pole
to balance,
Love delves into
mysterious crevices,
gently opens doors
and bows,
holds hands,
listens to the wise
and cries.
Love looks young
then old then young again.
It feels crushed
between opposing forces
then forces itself
to live another day.
Its heart is exposed,
alive.
As the cool predawn air
curls around its extremities,
and the day's virgin light
awakens,
Love looks in your eyes
and kisses your mouth,
touches your body
and never wants to depart.

We crane our necks
and look up at Love.
The day's heat has come
and now wanes.
Love looks crumpled
on that wire.
Will it fall and tumble
topsy-turvy
to a tumultuous end?
Somehow the air currents
settle,
the waving wire regains
its stature.
Our collective sigh
sends reverberations
upward.
Love glances down
and smiles.
Looking inward,
regaining balance,
Love searches out the Way.

Ordering Coffee

He chats while ordering coffee.
His hip was replaced
but he's doing great
he says.
I hear chuckling
and thanks
as he prepares to leave.
Then,
limping away,
he gazes inward
at his prodigious loneliness,
and every step forward
is heroic.

The Tympani

The tympani
of distress
undress their reverberations.
Pounding sounds
wound around
your physiognomy,
tighten tighten
until the screwheads
pop off
and your eyes disappear
inside your head.
Percussion,
the energy driving
the symphony,
makes your heart
beat twice,
makes you twinge
and wince
and cringe.
Unable to change
the harmony
you recoil.
You absorb
the clash.

When You Look Behind

When you look
behind,
when your head
tweaks to the right
or left,
you see winter
in Minnesota.
It is white and cold
with diamond-studded
glitterings.
The sky is so blue,
the sun is so bright,
but it is so damn cold.
You look behind,
place your hands
on your hips,
feel the warmth
of your down jacket,
your fingers buried in mittens,
your memories buried
in a handsome
landscape.

You Told Me

You told me
you enjoy being alone.
Our worlds and orbits
flame far away,
they rotate in different
sectors of the universe
but I hold on
to a lifeline.
When I see your face
and the spirit
behind it,
when I see your shape
my imagination and pulse
quicken.
Our connection is ephemeral,
something I inspect,
reflect upon,
absorb and pursue.
You told me
and smiled.
I smiled back
because I am
an intergalactic
explorer.

Looking Backward

Looking backward
over his shoulder
at the artwork
hanging in the gallery
he imagines himself
frolicking inside a painting,
powering himself
with elbows pumping,
breathing deeply,
struggling to reach
the pinnacle,
feeling and smelling
the fragrant breeze,
feeling the emptiness too
of a goal attained.
In his youthful
exuberance,
running down becomes
the trial.
Amidst the green
coercive chlorophyll
he jets downward
pursuing
he knows not what,
legs and body
propelled forward,
flailing momentarily
only to recapture
equilibrium.

Downward downward
panting as the path
flattens,
slowing to a trot,
he stops and beams,
looking up at
where he's been.

Other paintings
catch his eye-
a garden shimmering
with blends of oils,
a winter road
sending biting shivers
down his spine.

Before he leaves
he takes one last glance
at his youth,
then pushes himself
forward.

A Door

A door
with a bright burnished handle,
waited,
a tiny undefined door.
Can anyone fit through?
Squeaky smoothness
filled the air,
breeziness easiness.
Suddenly a form emerged-
hair, face, body, feet,
a feat defying rules.
That door,
so forgiving,
benign and malignant,
opened
letting light through
letting life through,
merging worlds
creating sounds.
Now the door has closed.

A Siren

A siren pierces
the evening calm.
Did a man have a
heart attack?
Did he feel
incredible pain?
Did a distracted driver
make a momentary
mistake?
Did she veer to the
right and hit
a parked car
or a pedestrian?
Is there death
or injury?
Does the patient in the ambulance
require surgery?
What skills and equipment
do the doctors utilize?
Who makes the call
to a family member or friend?
A siren
is a harbinger of questions.

A Sparkling Whiff

The stomach
rumbles.
An aroma
rises in
through nostrils.
It is the curved
smooth white petal
of an indifferent rose.
A hand
with attentive fingers
reaches out
to pull in
the freshest
of blossoms,
to pull it
up and in,
to smell it
deeply.
The stomach rumbles.
The floral image
fades and
dissipates
leaving a
sparkling whiff.

A Student

When I saw her this morning
as I walked into class
I smiled and said hello.
She looked at me
but didn't say a word.
Later,
circulating around the room,
she stared into my eyes
and didn't say a word.
I wondered why.
Her eyes are bright,
her braces-filled mouth
glistens,
her curved ears
reach forward.

A Wintery Place

The world can be
a wintery place.
The cold wind can
pierce your crevices,
shoot its razorblade edge
down into naive
unsuspecting warmth.
You are affected,
your feet shift
as temporary imbalance
unlocks logic.
You will tumble
or regain a stronger hold.
Winter can be cruel,
freezing all exposed
extremities.
Pull down that hat
farther!
Hunch your shoulders,
block out the openings,
bend your knees
and spread your feet.
The blizzard will devour you
unless you fight.

Bird Song

The bird sits so knowingly
high on the thin black wire.
Her head tilts back
chirping an indecipherable code,
beseeching a faraway partner.
Or is gladness erupting from
her heart giving sound to feeling.
The bird swoops and vanishes.

Peering Into the Past

Peering into the past,
peeking around the corner,
spying documents of youth.
It was a turbulent world
at twenty-one.
So much knowledge!
So little knowledge!
Manipulating and fondling
words,
shaping sentiment
into written shouts of distress,
wonder and tentative truth.
Oh, the full-flavored
beverage of inexperience.
These yellowed sheets
pour forth seeing,
touching dreaming.
Clear evidence of climbing
the onerous ladder
of life,
one long and separated rung
from the other.
Each step detailed and described,
painted from an inscrutable
palette.

Phil

Phil is dying.
He's in hospice care.
His wife Rayma called
last night.
This man has lived
his life consciously
to the very best
of his ability.
It's a cliché
but I am a witness
to it.
He has loved his family
and mourned
the pain of early losses.

Sitting across from Phil
for many years,
looking in his eyes,
listening to his words,
his soul expanded
to include me.
I feel blessed
to have shared
the intimate memories and feelings
of another man's life.
We laughed and cried
together
at his house or mine.
We greeted with joy

our children and our wives.
He would marvel
at how my sons had grown.

Now Phil is dying,
breathing his last breaths
of this world.
No more pounding out anger
or shaking out fear.
Now a quiet retreat
into oblivion's deep embrace.
He joins his mother,
the sweet woman
he longed to know longer.
He joins his father,
the terse man
who never reached out to him.

Adieu my friend.
As you pass away
you pass into
a secret chamber
in my Being,
populated by
the few people
I have truly
loved.

Questions

When a pen runs out
of ink,
does the cartridge feel
an ethereal satisfaction,
the sweet fruits of a life
well-lived?
Or is death drab,
unromantic,
corpse-producing,
wasting of flesh and blood?

She is the Captain

She asked why no poetry
was dedicated to her.
Why her figure
was never outlined
on the prow of a ship
crashing through waves.
She asked a good question.

Walking deep within
the caves and recesses
of experience and thought,
he eyes a light,
wonders at its source
wanders towards its warmth.
From dark to bright
his view adjusts
adapts.
Silhouettes dart helter skelter
and dissipate.
Insight occurs.

The ship appears
with white white billowy sails,
a flag whips up high
on an active breeze.
She is the captain
of this ship.
She is radiant.
He boards

and kisses each of her cheeks.
She is the captain.

The Sky

The sky
surprised me.
How can something
seen daily,
observed ignored,
sometimes relegated
to insignificance,
circle back,
expose its complex features,
like cobras
at the side of the road
in Cameroon,
become an intricate interplay
of clouds,
penetrating light,
kaleidoscopic colorings
causing a paradigm shift.
I am floating in that sky,
I am soaring in and out
with wave-like movement.
The sky,
enigmatic automatic
influential
Original.

Scratchings

Scratchings
etchings
slowly uncover,
present
an outline
of understanding.
Tiny divots,
unremarkable shavings
eat away at
the unknown,
the unwanted,
releasing
sense,
unleashing
history,
shouting,
like Moses
on a rock,
the truth.
Or
a silent wink,
acknowledgement
encouragement
to keep seeking.

F-Words

Five
fabulous fingers
found fun-filled feelings
foundered fumbled fell.
Five fingers finished
fourteen fables
figured fundamentals
followed phantoms.
Five fidgeting fingers
flipped flopped fainted.
Five formal fingers.
Five fallen fingers.
Free fresh friendly
fashionable fingers.
Fingers feel frazzled.
Fingers find favor.
Fingers flow fluidly
fruitfully famously.
Fortuitous fingers.
Philanthropic fingers.
Forgetful fingers.
Forest fragrant fingers.
Five fabulous fingers.
Five fictitious fingers.
Five.

Surprise

Surprise.
Living
without reflection.
Concentrating
on wisdom's immediate
sigh.
Creating
a natural response
to elucidate emancipate
laugh.
Afterward
acknowledgement.
What is out of the
ordinary?
Responses
invite new insight.
Turn my head
towards what I
did not expect.
Now.
Breath dissipates
into a molecular pool
of surprise.

The Surface

The surface said hello
The inside asked who you are
Outside was a cheerful countenance
Below was a clawing anxiety
Above confidence searched for expression
Within lay depression
Today the yellow sun illuminates and heats
Tonight red dreams rock the psyche
Sunrise means rotational commencement
Sunset ends our sense of turning
Surface inside outside below
Above within today tonight
Sunrise sunset

Peering Outward

Her lips part
in awe,
sensing the sun's
deliberate heat,
while stepping delicately
to the door.
Peering outward,
a pure breeze
bathes her breasts
and body,
belly thighs and
toes.
Tingles ripple,
they course north
and south.
Her eyes wide,
nostrils round,
saliva's spigot
opens.
After one more
slight shuffle
forward,
she glances east and west
smiling serenely.

Faults

He glanced from
left to right,
nervous.
These were his
younger years,
nothing seemed
stable.
Earthquakes within,
7.1 on the Richter
scale.
Have the aftershocks
stopped?
Where and how
he peered and appeared
mattered.
A pure fresh
breath of air
washed
shower-like
upon his upturned
face.
Those faults
have value.

Spectacles

Spectacles
Spectacular
Clarifying
Closeness
Dimming
Distances
Farsighted
Far-out
Reading
Relaxation
Print
Predominates
Understanding
Underscored
Nuances
Noticed
Text
Textures
Grammatical
Gradations
Voice
Voiced
Meaning
Meaningful
Spectacles
Spectacular

Look East

Worry is
a barbed spear
that stabs the heart.
It interrupts
regenerative rest.
It is poisonous venomous,
unconquerable,
it seems.
The fist of Tao
crashes down.
It grabs the bloody
snake from its
putrid root.
Smashed against
a rock
it dies.
Life is born anew.
A calm and fragrant
breeze
eases through the heart.
Worry is tamed,
confined and constrained.

That Lake

The aluminum craft
tuh, tuh, tuh'd
across the wide-open lake
while our young eyes
manufactured visions
of large fish,
sleek smooth scaled,
tugging on our lines
making us stand and stretch
reeling in reality.
Later in life,
real time creates
other noises:
puddles of pragmatism,
seas of circumstances,
oceans of circulation.
Glancing back momentarily,
remembering how we ensnared
those northern pike,
a breeze brushes past
unencumbered
fresh from that lake
nestled in memory.

My Swing

The wind stirred the leaves
above my head
as American Crows-
corvus brachyrhynchos-
looked down and considered me.
I was ready with my
playing partners
atop the rise.
I waggled professionally
and the crows quieted.
After my swing
the orange ball
spun toward the green.
It reached an apex
and descended
like a spherical genius,
like a mathematical
know-it-all.
There were two bounces
on the putting surface,
then the ball disappeared
into the hole.
It was a geometric anomaly,
athletic serendipity.
As I howled
from on high,
the crows were
oblivious.

Reluctance

Reluctance.
A want not to want
inevitable exposure
to others.
Eyes flit within
then a determined grin.
Mouth stretches down
forming a nervous frown.
Goaded.
A required
explosion of effort.
Correction.
Repetition.
Correction.
Sighing
semi-satisfied.

On Snow

Once,
when wonders ruled,
he dreamed-
a motor revving
in his heart.
He reached up,
his leather gloves
touching hope.
Extending his insulated frame
on indifferent snow,
eyes focused
on the stark blue sky,
alone,
surrounded by cold
slowly melting
frozen fear.

In Normandy

The frosty flowers bloom
in front of me
but are not real;
their crackled texture
evolving through time.
I walk in their abundance
surprised to be in Normandy
though I am not.
Now a voice calls out saying,
Pray for me my son.
A soul is here
but isn't.
Long years of a life
unseen.
This bond is real
it seems.
I climb a hill
to observe
the sail dotted sea,
encumbered
by a dream.

Hanukkah

Their eyes dart
towards sparks
and follow the flame
as it ignites
a solitary wick
that celebrates the day.
This yellow candle,
the shammas,
raises its sparkling head,
as we say the prayers,
then tips its fiery cap
towards the next one,
inflaming a ready red candle.
I see those eyes
reflecting light,
eager too for the presence
of presents.

Around the Corner

Around the corner
Away from the light of day
Where shadow carpets perception
A spark can ignite.

As you sit quietly
Separated and reflective
Abandoned by traditions
Fear permeates your soul.

You stare yourself in the face
You examine and reexamine
Every minute detail
Every possible outcome.

The sun does not rise or set around the corner
It is blind and deaf
But not heartless
It is roughly hewn and open.

What resides there
Belongs to you and no one else
It might be detested or abhorred by others
But you cherish it.

A Short Poem

A short poem
like a short person
always wonders
what would life
be like
if they were six foot three
or had
three more stanzas.

The Laugh

When he said
those few words
he looked at her face,
saw the smile,
heard the laugh,
and was glad
he said them.

Hands and Words

Her hand touched his
as they said goodbye.
He pulled to go,
but she held on
and squeezed;
their hands speaking
a different language
than their words.

The Booth

The booth is empty now.
Sugar spilled in crystalline randomness
lies on the table
amid the crumpled and stained napkin
that tidied his face.

He has baggy and puffy eyes
above an ample nose.
His cheeks and neck are full of gray spikes,
whiskers that long for a cool blade.
His mouth works hard,
opening closing,
chewing only interrupted by coughing,
when the combination of flavors join together
in an overwhelming rush of spice.
His flannel shirt,
frayed at the collar,
expands and contracts
with each bite of breakfast.
His hands are mirrors of his experiences,
like pottery with minute designs
intricately painted and fired to reflect
the wondrous complexity
of who he was and is.

I could not hear his voice,
jumbled by the cries, squeals,
and protestations of the generations
at the gathering.

Engrossed in my own meal,
I did not notice him walk past.
If I had,
I would have greeted the gentleman,
tried to make eye contact,
and thanked him for his contribution.

As the quick-wristed busboy
tidies up and wipes away
the evidence of that meal,
this man's image
remains in my mind.

Fear

Fear
Shaking
Unable to advance
Spinning inwardly
Yelping dog-like
Reaching out
From a tornado
Whipped back
Smacked
By fear

Searching

Searching.
His hand reached out,
extended.
Match points flash points
sizzled from his fingertips.
The sparks,
shooting stars
illuminating the
murky heavens,
rushed sperm-like
to fertilize the egg.
Cold cool warm warmer hot.
Hot and fabulous
and passionate
like love.
Then relaxation.
After,
irked by wonderment,
busting loose again,
eradicating complacency.
Searching.

Contained

Contained
within,
coursing through
veins and arteries
the passion pulses.
He steps on
tabletops,
prances,
stretching fingers
up,
snapping them
down.
Sitting calmly,
engrossed in
grotesque details,
a beautiful woman
walks by.
He shifts from
his seat,
grabs her waist and hand,
dances in circular swerves,
laughs and laughs.
Within.
Contained.

Peaks

On a shadowed shelf,
the porch of a stone-faced lodge,
looking westward
at magnificent mountains,
enormous sun-bathed sentries
stand guard,
reflecting the eastern blaze.
Later,
walking leaning forward
stepping up a steep paved road,
different sentries
watch my passage.
I pause panting,
salute their opulence
their sheer size.
Evergreens and granite abound,
the mountainsides appear smooth
from snow at another season
melting joyriding
down down.
Now,
back on the shelf
as the afternoon shadow narrows,
my gaze once more embraces
peaks.

Goodbye

I turn
to look
over my shoulder.
The beginning
happened a
moment ago.
The end lies
just in front.
Goodbye.
My father
will die soon.
As a boy
I reached up
to him.
He didn't really
see me.
The end is
within view.
Hello becomes goodbye.
Mystery and unknowns
melt into knowns and
mysteries.
The day after the end
is a beginning
too.

Hmm...

I.

The celebration begins.
Smiles
Surrounded by objects
Valueless valuables
Thanks and hugs and best wishes.
I have so much.

II.

Standing before the crowd
Love in hearts and eyes
Christian benediction
Before a god and Jesus.
Oh happiness!
A pearl shared
Developed from the depths
Like hands held together.

III.

Life in the world
Lucky materialists
Insipid joyfulness.
It is so much
To offer so little.

Time

Time twirls,
spins creating
concentric circles
whirlpools mirages.
Stepping gently,
tiptoeing,
with index finger
brought to trembling lips
to hush the rush,
deceleration occurs,
a slowing down,
an opportunity to peak around,
to glimpse your surroundings,
to see beyond what is
in front of your eyes,
to delve deeply into spirit,
to understand who and what
lives inside.
The hands of time wave on,
the turning of Earth,
so incredibly fast.
But all we feel is calm.
Craggy mountains
beckon to be climbed,
cold breezes freeze the spine,
but the heart pumps on,
and warmth circulates.
Displacement replacement,
emptiness fulfillment,

spontaneous eruption
spontaneous tranquility,
as time ticks,
picks its victims,
stretches their hearts
across canvas souls.
And the painter approaches
brushes in hand, une artiste,
we trust her originality,
the truth of her strokes,
Cézanne-like though
uniquely her own.
Ah, the luxuriousness
of fulfillment,
the wink of an eye.
Time
Timeliness
In time
one time.
Our time.

A Nine Eleven Memory

Many years ago
jets as weapons
crashed and burned
crashed and churned
the Trade Towers to dust.
Yesterday,
sitting in a synagogue,
watching and listening
to the rabbi read the Torah,
tradition whispered in my ear.
This morning,
my bicycle,
miles from ideology,
carried me
on a journey,
circumnavigated
all the indecisions
of the road.
Now,
the past has sublimed
into what comes next.

A Swoop A Quiver

A swoop
a quiver
standing on
a precipice
staring hard
down into blackness
squeezing your eyes
shut then open
attempting to
delineate
form or
structure.
What appears
below
flitters and
flickers
like a tiny
candle flame
emitting a
fragrant essence
which tickles
titillates
touches
bewilders.

Assets and Liabilities

As I reached for
my skates,
noticing the reflective
blades,
I dreamed of excellence,
of digging for the puck
in the corner,
or skating backward
quickly smoothly elegantly
like Bobby Orr.
Standing,
walking haphazardly
toward the rink,
fantasy evaporated
as my Bauers touched
real life,
unadulterated me,
who I am
in this realm.
Today
I am surrounded
by hockey
surrounded by
my assets and liabilities.

Betsey

(Inspired by a former student)

She is nutty,
a roasted organic
almond.
She is forgetful.
I left my lunch ticket
in the classroom
she says.
She talks too much,
says whatever is
on her mind
regardless of
the situation.
But she calls me
Superstar
even after I speak
firmly to her.
She is a nut,
peanut walnut cashew.
During P.E.
she gets smacked
in the face
by another boy's head
while playing kickball.
I see the fear and pain
on her face.
It makes my heart
ache.
I try to hug away

the pain.
She is a nut.

Blade of Truth

The surface,
exterior,
could be pocked
by tree stumps
or irrigation ditches.
It could be marked
or delineated
by buoys and boats
upon an undulating
unending series
of tides.
But below
lies the true essence,
the unbending
naked steel,
the indefatigable
blade of truth.